The Internet
FOR DUMMIES®

Pocket Edition

by John R. Levine, Carol Baroudi, and Margaret Levine Young

Windows Millennium preview by Andy Rathbone

IDG BOOKS WORLDWIDE

IDG Books Worldwide, Inc.
An International Data Group Company

Foster City, CA ✦ Chicago, IL ✦ Indianapolis, IN ✦ New York, NY

The Internet For Dummies®, Pocket Edition

Published by
IDG Books Worldwide, Inc.
An International Data Group Company
919 E. Hillsdale Blvd.
Suite 400
Foster City, CA 94404
www.idgbooks.com (IDG Books Worldwide Web Site)
www.dummies.com (Dummies Press Web Site)

Copyright © 2000 IDG Books Worldwide, Inc. All rights reserved. No part of this book, including interior design, cover design, and icons, may be reproduced or transmitted in any form, by any means (electronic, photocopying, recording, or otherwise) without the prior written permission of the publisher.

Library of Congress Catalog Control Number: 00-104208

ISBN: 0-7645-0766-4

10 9 8 7 6 5 4 3 2 1

1S/SV/QT/QQ/IN

For general information on IDG Books Worldwide's books in the U.S., please call our Consumer Customer Service department at 800-762-2974. For reseller information, including discounts and premium sales, please call our Reseller Customer Service department at 800-434-3422.

LIMIT OF LIABILITY/DISCLAIMER OF WARRANTY: THE PUBLISHER AND AUTHOR HAVE USED THEIR BEST EFFORTS IN PREPARING THIS BOOK. THE PUBLISHER AND AUTHOR MAKE NO REPRESENTATIONS OR WARRANTIES WITH RESPECT TO THE ACCURACY OR COMPLETENESS OF THE CONTENTS OF THIS BOOK AND SPECIFICALLY DISCLAIM ANY IMPLIED WARRANTIES OF MERCHANTABILITY OR FITNESS FOR A PARTICULAR PURPOSE. THERE ARE NO WARRANTIES WHICH EXTEND BEYOND THE DESCRIPTIONS CONTAINED IN THIS PARAGRAPH. NO WARRANTY MAY BE CREATED OR EXTENDED BY SALES REPRESENTATIVES OR WRITTEN SALES MATERIALS. THE ACCURACY AND COMPLETENESS OF THE INFORMATION PROVIDED HEREIN AND THE OPINIONS STATED HEREIN ARE NOT GUARANTEED OR WARRANTED TO PRODUCE ANY PARTICULAR RESULTS, AND THE ADVICE AND STRATEGIES CONTAINED HEREIN MAY NOT BE SUITABLE FOR EVERY INDIVIDUAL. NEITHER THE PUBLISHER NOR AUTHOR SHALL BE LIABLE FOR ANY LOSS OF PROFIT OR ANY OTHER COMMERCIAL DAMAGES, INCLUDING BUT NOT LIMITED TO SPECIAL, INCIDENTAL, CONSEQUENTIAL, OR OTHER DAMAGES.

Trademarks: For Dummies, Dummies Man, A Reference for the Rest of Us!, The Dummies Way, Dummies Daily, and related trade dress are registered trademarks or trademarks of IDG Books Worldwide, Inc. in the United States and other countries, and may not be used without written permission. All other trademarks are the property of their respective owners. IDG Books Worldwide is not associated with any product or vendor mentioned in this book.

is a registered trademark under exclusive license to IDG Books Worldwide, Inc. from International Data Group, Inc.

Table of Contents

Introduction 1

Part 1: Getting Down to E-Mail 3
   Identifiying Your Address 3
   Managing Mail 4
   Finding E-Mail Addresses 5
   Eating Spam 5
   Catching a Virus 6
   Mastering Mailing Lists 7
      Subscribing and posting to a mailing list 8
      Replying to a mailing list message 8
      Finding interesting lists 10
   Protecting Yourself on the Web 10

Part 2: Zipping Around the Web 15
   Keeping Your Favorites Close at Mouse 15
      Bookmarking with Netscape 16
      Choosing favorites with Internet Explorer .. 17
   Going Site-Seeing in a Hurry 19
      Axe the pictures 19
      Go for the cache 20
      Open multiple windows 22
   Putting It on Paper — Printing 22

Part 3: Playing Olly, Olly, Information Free! 25
   Developing a Basic Search Strategy 25

Locating Popular Search Engines 26
   Yahoo! 27
   Google and AltaVista 28
   Other popular search engines 29

Part 4: Mastering Netiquette 31
Read Before You Write 31
   Advice you probably didn't hear from
   your mom 32
Check Your Spelling and Punctuation 33
Don't Abuse Mailing Lists 33
Edit Yourself 34
Don't Embarrass Someone 35
Keep Your Signature Short 35
Don't Get Attached 36
Don't Flame 36
Don't Send Chain Letters or Spam 37
Don't Be a Glutton 38
Bone Up on Cybercafé Etiquette 39
Make Your Web Site User Friendly 40

Part 5: Welcoming You to the Windows Millennium 43
What Are Windows and Windows Me? 44
What Does Windows Do? 45
How Does Windows Me Affect My
Older Programs? 48
Should I Bother Using Windows Me? 49
   Upgrading from Windows 95 49
   Upgrading from Windows 3.1 50
   Upgrading from Windows 98 52
Bracing Yourself (And Your Computer) for
Windows Me 52

Introduction

The Internet For Dummies, Pocket Edition, is the perfect tool for the novice surfer. If you're brand new to the online world, this book offers all the essential tools to get you started. Even if you already have some basic skills for tooling around the Web, you're bound to find some hints along the way that just make life easier.

This book has five parts. Each part stands on its own, so you can begin reading wherever you like:

- **Part 1: Getting Down to E-Mail:** This part tells you everything you need to know to start sending and receiving e-mail, join a mailing list, and keep yourself safe on the Web.

- **Part 2: Zipping Around the Web:** This part provides the tools you need to surf the Internet quickly and efficiently.

- **Part 3: Playing Olly, Olly, Information Free!:** This part shows you how to identify and use Internet tools that can help you develop an effective search strategy.

- **Part 4: Mastering Netiquette:** This part helps you cultivate good manners for the electronic world.

- **Part 5: Welcoming You to the Windows Millennium:** An added bonus from IDG Books Worldwide and author Andy Rathbone, this part covers the basics of Microsoft's latest and greatest.

Occasionally, you'll notice little pictures off to the left-hand side of a paragraph or sidebar. We call these *icons,* and they're meant to highlight important information. The icons we use are as follows:

The bull's-eye indicates a nifty little shortcut or time-saver that you may want to employ.

This icon is a signal that the information is worth making an extra effort to remember.

Gaack! We found out about these things the hard way! Don't let it happen to you!

This icon highlights geeky stuff you may or may not find interesting. You decide whether you want to read it.

Part 1
Getting Down to E-Mail

∙∙∙∙∙∙∙∙∙∙∙∙∙∙∙∙∙∙∙∙∙∙∙∙∙∙∙∙∙∙∙∙

In This Part
▶ Recognizing your own address
▶ Locating your friends' e-mail addresses
▶ Dealing with junk mail and viruses
▶ Using mailing lists
▶ Staying safe and secure on the Web

∙∙∙∙∙∙∙∙∙∙∙∙∙∙∙∙∙∙∙∙∙∙∙∙∙∙∙∙∙∙∙∙

*T*he Internet began as a way to share ideas and information, so it's only natural that you'd like to share your ideas and information with other people. This chapter covers all the information you need to send e-mails, filter out junk mail, avoid nasty viruses, and join mailing lists to share your interest in everything from kookaburras to nuclear medicine — staying safe all the while.

Identifying Your Address

Everyone with e-mail access to the Net has at least one e-mail address, which is the cyberspace equivalent of a postal address or a phone number. Internet mail addresses have two parts, separated by an @ (the at sign). The part before the @ is the mailbox, which is (roughly speaking) your personal name, and the part after that is the *domain,* usually the name of the company that supplies your Internet service (this company is an Internet service provider, commonly abbreviated as ISP), such as aol.com.

The mailbox is usually your user name, the name your ISP assigns to your account. If you're lucky, you get to choose your user name; in other cases, ISPs standardize user names, and you get what you get. The domain name for ISPs in the United States usually ends with three letters that give you a clue to what kind of place it is. Commercial organizations end with .com. Colleges and universities end with .edu, networking organizations end with .net, U.S. government sites end with .gov, military sites end with .mil, and organizations that don't fall into any of those categories (like non-profits) end with .org. Outside the United States, domains usually end with a country code, such as .fr for France.

Managing Mail

After you've read an e-mail message, you can do a bunch of different things with it: throw it away, reply to it, forward it to other people, or file it. If you don't tell your mail program what to do to a message, the message either stays in your mailbox for later perusal, or sometimes gets saved to a read-messages folder. If your mail program automatically saves messages in a read-messages, Sent, or Outbox folder, be sure to go through the folder every week or so; otherwise, it becomes enormous and unmanageable.

When you reply to a message, most mail programs fill in the Subject field with the letters *Re:* (short for *regarding*) and the subject of the message to which you're replying. When you reply, look carefully at the To: line your mail program has filled out for you. If the To: list isn't correct, you can move the cursor to it and edit it as necessary. Most e-mail programs begin your reply message with the content of the message to which you're replying. Begin by including it and then edit the text to just the relevant material. If you don't give some context to people who get a great deal of e-mail, your reply makes no sense.

Finding E-Mail Addresses

Locating the e-mail addresses of friends and colleagues can be a chore. Following are some suggestions of easy ways to track down those people to whom you want to send e-mail:

- **Yahoo! People Search:** Go to people.yahoo.com and try its e-mail search. If you want other people to be able to find you, list yourself here, too.
- **WhoWhere?:** Go to www.whowhere.lycos.com, enter the name of the person you want to find, and click the WhoWhere FIND button.
- **Alumni directories:** Colleges and universities are creating Web sites to help promote themselves, and many are choosing to list some sort of alumni directory.

Eating Spam

The word *spam* on the Internet means thousands of copies of the same piece of unwanted e-mail, sent to either individual e-mail accounts or Usenet newsgroups. The message usually consists of unsavory advertising for get-rich-quick schemes, or even pornographic offers. Spam, unfortunately, is a major problem on the Internet because sleazy business entrepreneurs and occasional political lowlifes have decided that it's the ideal way to advertise.

> **WARNING**
>
> Many *spammers* (the technical term for people who send spam) include a line that instructs you how to get off their lists by sending them an e-mail with instructions to remove your name. Don't bother: Spammers' remove lists never work. In fact, they're usually a method for verifying that your address is real, and they're likely to send you *more* spam, not less.

Catching a Virus

Viruses have been around the Internet for a long time. Currently, most viruses are spread through files that are sent via e-mail, as attachments to mail messages.

> **REMEMBER**
>
> The text of a plain text message can't contain a virus, but attachments can, and sometimes do. For the virus to work (that is, for it to operate, infect your computer, and send copies of itself out to other people via e-mail), you need to run it. In most e-mail programs, programs contained in attachments don't run until you click them — so *don't* open programs that come from people you don't know. Don't even open attachments from people you *do* know if you weren't expecting to receive them.

> **WARNING:** If you use Microsoft's Outlook Express 5.0 or Outlook with Windows 98, the situation is more dire. Outlook (which comes with Microsoft Office) opens attachments as soon as you view the message. Outlook Express provides a *preview pane* that displays a file and its attachments before you click it at all. Luckily, Microsoft has provided a patch, which is available at www.microsoft.com/security/Bulletins/ms99-032.asp.

Mastering Mailing Lists

The point of a mailing list is simple. The list has its own special e-mail address, and anything someone sends to that address is sent to all the people on the list. Because these people in turn often respond to the messages, the result is a running conversation. Mailing lists fall into three categories:

- **Discussion:** Every subscriber can post a message. These lists lead to freewheeling discussions and can include a certain number of off-topic messages.

- **Moderated:** A moderator reviews each message before it gets distributed. The moderator can stop unrelated, redundant, or clueless postings from wasting everyone's time.

- **Announcement-only:** Only the moderator posts messages.

Subscribing and posting to a mailing list

Most lists are run by programs called *list servers* or *mailing list managers*. You get on or off most mailing lists by sending an e-mail message to the list server program. Because a program is reading the message, it has to be spelled and formatted exactly right. Other lists are managed by programs with Web interfaces — to get on or off a list, you go to the Web site and click links.

Some lists encourage new subscribers to send in a message introducing themselves and briefly describing their interests. Others don't. Don't send anything until you have something to say. When you're ready, try sending something by mailing a message to the list address, which is the same as the name of the list with the domain name added — `dandruff-l@bluesuede.org`, for example. On popular lists, you may begin to get back responses within a few minutes of sending a message.

Replying to a mailing list message

When you receive an interesting message from a list you're going to want to respond to it. Depending on how the list owner set up the list software, your answer either goes just to the person who sent the original message or to the entire list. About half the list owners set things up so that replies automatically go to just the person who sent the original message. The other half set things up so that replies go to the entire list. In messages coming from the list, the mailing-list software automatically sets the `Reply-To:` header line to the address to which replies should be sent.

Posting protocol for the savvy mailing list member

The last thing you want when you subscribe to a list is to look like you have no clue what you're doing. Here are some handy tips for looking sharp on a list:

- **Don't send anything to a new list until you've been reading it for a week:** You can discern what topics people really discuss, the tone of the list, and so on. You also get a fair idea about which topics people are tired of. The classic newcomer gaffe is to subscribe to a list and immediately send a message asking a dumb question that isn't really germane to the topic and that was beaten to death three days earlier.

- **Don't send a message directly to the list asking to subscribe or unsubscribe:** This type of message should go to the list manager, where the list maintainer (human or robotic) can handle your request, not to the list itself, where all the other subscribers can see your mistake.

- **Don't send "enriched" formatted messages, attachments, or anything other than text:** Many e-mail programs don't handle non-text, so send only plain text messages.

- **Don't waste everyone's time by posting a response on the list when you don't like what another person is posting:** The only thing more annoying than a stupid posting is a response complaining about it. Instead, e-mail the person privately and tell him to stop, or e-mail the list manager and ask that person to intervene.

TIP

Fortunately, you're in charge. When you start to create a reply, your mail program should show you the address to which it's replying. If you don't like the address it's using, change the address. While you're fixing the recipient's address, you may also want to alter the Subject: line. After a few rounds of replies to replies to replies, the topic of discussion often wanders away from the original topic. At that point, changing the subject to better describe what's really under discussion is very helpful.

Finding interesting lists

Tens of thousands of lists reside on the Internet. For a huge, searchable list of lists, check out one of the mailing list directory sites, such as the Liszt (bad pun) site, at www.liszt.com, or Topica, at www.topica.com. You can search for lists that include a word or phrase in the name or one-line description of the list. After you locate a list that sounds interesting, Liszt or Topica can tell you how to subscribe.

Protecting Yourself on the Web

The Internet is a funny place. Although it seems completely anonymous, it's not. People used to have Internet usernames that bore some resemblance to their true identity, which gave a fairly traceable route to an actual person. Today, with the phenomenon of screen names and multiple e-mail addresses, revealing your identity is definitely optional.

> **WARNING:** Don't use your full name or ever provide your name, address, and phone number over the Net to someone you don't know. Never believe anyone who says that he is from "AOL tech support" or some such authority and asks you for your password. No legitimate entity will ever ask you for your password. Be especially careful about disclosing information about kids. In the online world, it seems that a whole bunch of people are extremely interested in who you are, what sites you visit, and, most especially, what you buy. Here are a few hints to control how much or how little info you give them:

- **Cookies:** To enhance your online experience, the makers of Web browsers have invented a type of special message, called a *cookie*, that lets a Web site recognize you when you revisit that site. The site stores this info on your machine to make your next visit to the site smoother. Cookie files usually have the name cookie associated with them — `cookies.txt` on Windows and `MagicCookie` on a Mac, for example. You can delete your cookie files — your browser will create a new, empty one. Modern browsers can tell you about cookies and ask you whether to accept them as servers offer them to you. Contrary to rumor, cookie files can't get other information from your hard disk, give you a bad haircut, or otherwise mess up your life. They collect only information that the browser tells them about.

- **History files:** In addition to the cookie file, Internet Explorer keeps a history file of where you've been on the Web. (Look in your Windows folder for a subfolder called History.) If anyone other than you uses your computer, you may want to delete its contents after your use.

- **Encryption:** You can guarantee security when you make purchases over the Internet by using *encryption*. Encryption is high-tech-ese for encoding — just like with a secret decoder ring. Encryption is the virtual envelope that defies prying eyes.

The Net is a wonderful place, and meeting new people and making new friends is one of the big attractions. However, though relatively rare, horrible things have happened to a few people who have taken their Internet encounters into real life. You can safely meet people via the Internet if you simply use common sense when you set up a meeting with a Net friend:

- **Talk to the person on the phone before you agree to meet:** If anything makes you feel nervous, don't meet in person.

- **Depending on the context, try to check the person out a little:** If you've met in a newsgroup or chat room, ask others you know whether they know this person. (Women, ask another woman before meeting a man.)

- **Meet in a well-lit public place, and take a friend or two with you.**

- **Take a parent with you, if you're a kid:** Never, ever meet someone from the Net without your parents' explicit consent.

Your credit card, please

When you fill out a form on a Web page, you may need to provide information that you'd prefer not be made public — your credit card number, for example. Not to worry! Modern browsers can encrypt the information you send and receive to and from a secure Web server. You can tell when a page was received encrypted from the Web server by an icon in the lower-left corner of your browser window. If the little lock appears open, the page was not encrypted. If the little lock is locked, encryption is on. Typed data in forms on secure pages are almost always sent encrypted as well, making it impossible for anyone to snoop on your secrets as they pass through the Net.

Part 2
Zipping Around the Web

- -

In This Part

▶ Using bookmarks, Internet style
▶ Traveling the Web in the express lane
▶ Printing from the Internet

- -

Most Internet users have two major complaints about trying to use this technology. The first is how difficult it is to remember their favorite sites. Type in one wrong letter, and the site seems to be lost forever. The second — and this one is big — is the length of time Web pages take to load. Even people with high-speed connections still spend a good deal of time waiting for Web pages to load on their screen. This chapter provides remedies for both complaints (well, at least it offers tips to ease the pain). For good measure, we also tell you how to print the good stuff you find online.

Keeping Your Favorites Close at Mouse

Web browser-makers allow you to easily remember your favorite Web sites without having to repeatedly type in the *URL* (Internet address). Basically, your browser lets you mark a Web page and adds its URL to a list. Later, when you want to go back, you just go to your list and pick the page you want. Netscape calls these saved Web addresses *bookmarks;* Internet Explorer calls them *Favorites.*

Bookmarking with Netscape

Netscape bookmarks lurk under the Bookmarks Quick File button, which is located to the left of the Location box, below the Back button on the toolbar (in Netscape 4.x). To add a bookmark for a Web page, choose Communicator⇨Bookmarks⇨Add Bookmark or press Ctrl+D. The bookmarks appear as entries on the menu that appears when you click the Bookmarks Quick File button. To go to one of the pages on your bookmark list, just choose its entry from this menu.

Because all these bookmarks are "live," you can go to any of them by clicking them. (You can leave this window open while you move around the Web in other browser windows.) You can also add separator lines and submenus to organize your bookmarks and make the individual menus less unwieldy. Submenus look like folders in the Bookmarks window.

In the Bookmarks window in Netscape 4.x, choose File⇨New Separator to add a separator line and File⇨New Folder to add a new submenu. (Netscape asks you to type the name of the submenu before it creates the folder.) You can then drag the bookmarks, separators, and folders up and down to where you want them in the Bookmarks window. Drag an item to a folder to put it in that folder's submenu, and double-click a folder to display or hide that submenu. Any changes you make in the Bookmarks window are reflected immediately on the Bookmarks Quick File menu. When you're done fooling with your bookmarks, choose File⇨Close or press Ctrl+W to close the Bookmarks window.

> **WARNING:** Netscape preloads your bookmark window with pages they'd like you to look at, but feel free to delete them if your tastes are different from theirs.

Netscape also has a cool feature that enables you to see which of your bookmarks have been updated since you last looked at them. Open the Bookmarks window and then choose View⇨Update Bookmarks from the menu in the Bookmarks window. You see a little box asking which bookmarks you want to check. Click the Start Checking button. When Netscape finishes checking the Web pages on your bookmark list, it displays a message telling you how many have changed. The icons in the Bookmarks window reveal which pages have changed:

- The ones with little sparkles have new material.
- The ones with question marks are the ones Netscape isn't sure about.
- The ones that look normal haven't changed.

Choosing favorites with Internet Explorer

Internet Explorer uses a system similar to Netscape's, although it calls the saved pages favorites rather than bookmarks: You can add the current page to your Favorites folder and then look at and organize your Favorites folder. To add the current page to your Favorites folder, choose Favorites⇨Add to Favorites from the menu. To see your Favorites folder, choose Favorites➪Organize Favorites from the menu. Internet Explorer also has a Favorites button on the toolbar that displays your list of Favorites down the left side of your Internet Explorer window.

Exactly how the Favorites folder works depends on which version of Internet Explorer you're running. You can create subfolders in the Favorites folder so that you can store different types of files in different folders. To create a folder, click the Create New Folder button in 4.0 (the button with the yellow folder with a little sparkle, near the upper-right corner of the window) or the Create Folder button in 5.0. To move an item in the Favorites window into a folder, click the item, click the Move or Move to Folder button, and select the folder to move it to. You can see the contents of a folder by double-clicking it. When you finish organizing your favorite items, click the Close button.

In Internet Explorer 5.0, you can make pages available when you're not connected to the Internet by clicking on the page in the Favorites window and then clicking the Make available offline check box. Internet Explorer immediately fetches the page to your disk and refetches it from time to time when you're connected so that you can view the page offline when you click it.

> If you make several pages available offline, your browser spends a great deal of time keeping them up-to-date. When you no longer need to browse a page offline, uncheck its Make available offline box or remove it from Favorites altogether.

The folders you create in the Organize Favorites window appear on your F<u>a</u>vorites menu and the items you put in the folders appear on submenus. To return to a Web page you've added to your Favorites folder, just choose it from the F<u>a</u>vorites menu. In Windows 95/98, the Favorites folder usually appears on your Start menu. Choose Start➪F<u>a</u>vorites and then choose items from the menu. If the item is a Web page, your browser fires up and (if you're connected to the Internet) displays the Web page.

Going Site-Seeing in a Hurry

Chances are you probably spend a great deal of time wishing that the process of getting to stuff on the Web was faster. Here are a handful of tricks you can use to try to speed things up.

Axe the pictures

You can save quite a bit of time by skipping the pictures when you're browsing the Web. True, the pages don't look as snazzy, but they load like the wind. If you decide that you want to see the missing pictures after all, you can still do so.

In Netscape Navigator: Choose <u>E</u>dit➪Pr<u>e</u>ferences menu to display the Preference dialog box, click the Advanced category, and uncheck the <u>A</u>utomatically load images check box. This change tells Netscape to load only the text part of Web pages, which is small, and to hold off on the images, which are large. At every place on the page where an image should go, Netscape displays a box with three colored shapes. To see a particular image, click the three-shape box with the right mouse button and choose <u>L</u>oad Image from the menu that appears.

In Internet Explorer: You can tell Internet Explorer 4.0 and 5.0 not to bother loading images by choosing View➪Internet Options from the menu (Tools➪Internet Options in 5.0), clicking the Advanced tab, and scrolling down to the Multimedia section. If a checkmark or X appears in the Show pictures box, click in the box to remove the checkmark or X. Then click OK. Where pictures usually appear, you see a little box with three shapes in it. If you want to see a particular picture, right-click the little box and choose Show Picture from the menu that appears.

Go for the cache

When Netscape or Internet Explorer retrieves a page you have asked to see, it stores the page on your disk. If you ask for the same page again five minutes later, the program doesn't have to retrieve the page again — it can reuse the copy it already has. If you tell the program not to load images, for example, you get a fair number of them anyway because they've already been downloaded.

The space your browser uses to store pages is called its *cache* (pronounced "cash" because it's French and gives your cache more cachet). The more space you tell your browser to use for its cache, the faster pages appear the second time you look at them.

In Netscape Navigator: To set the size of the Netscape cache, follow these steps:

   1. Choose Edit➪Preferences from the menu.

   You see the Preferences dialog box.

   2. Double-click the Advanced category and click the Cache category.

The Disk Cache box shows the maximum size of the cache in kilobytes (K): Set Disk Cache to at least 4096 K (that is, 4MB). Set it to a higher number if you have a large hard disk with loads of free space.

3. **Click OK.**

In Internet Explorer: To set the size of the Internet Explorer 4.0 or 5.0 cache, follow these steps:

1. **Choose View➪Internet Options from the menu (Tools➪Internet Options in 5.0).**

    You see the Internet Options dialog box.

2. **Click the General tab.**

3. **Click the Settings button in the Temporary Internet files box.**

    You see the Settings dialog box, with information about the cache. *Note:* Many versions of Internet Explorer never call it a cache — guess they don't speak French.

4. **Click the slider on the Amount of disk space to use or Maximum size line and move it to about 10 percent.**

    If you have tons of empty disk space, you can slide it rightward to 20 percent. If you're short on space, move it leftward to 1 percent or 2 percent.

5. **Click OK twice.**

> **REMEMBER:** If you rarely exit your browser, remember that the pages your browser has cached aren't reloaded from the Web (they're taken from your disk) until you reload them. If you want to make sure that you're getting fresh pages, reload pages that you think may have changed since you last visited.

Open multiple windows

Netscape Navigator and Internet Explorer can have several Web browser windows open at a time. To display a page in a new window, click a link with the right mouse button and select Open in New Window from the menu that pops up. To close a window, click the little X box at the top right of the window frame, or press Alt+F4, the standard close-window shortcut.

You can also create a new window without following a link. Press Ctrl+N or choose File⇨New⇨Navigator Window (in Netscape 4.x) or File⇨New⇨Window (in Internet Explorer 4.0 or 5.0).

Putting It on Paper — Printing

To print a page from Netscape or Internet Explorer, just click the Print button on the toolbar, press Ctrl+P, or choose File⇨Print. Reformatting the page to print it can take awhile, so patience is a virtue. Fortunately, each browser displays a progress window to let you know how it's doing.

TIP: If the page you want to print uses *frames* (a technique that divides the browser window into subareas that can scroll and update separately), click in the part of the window you want to print before printing. Otherwise, you're likely to get the outermost frame, which usually just has a title and some buttons.

Part 3
Playing Olly, Olly, Information Free!

● ●

In This Part
▶ Building a search technique
▶ Finding useful search engines

● ●

You're probably wondering how to find all this great stuff out there on the Net. Well, you can start by reading this chapter, which introduces you to various ways to search for something on the Net.

Developing a Basic Search Strategy

When searching the Net, your best bet is to begin with one of the Web's many *search engines* (a fancy name for programs that search for information). You use them all in more or less the same way:

1. **Start your Web browser, such as Netscape or Internet Explorer.**
2. **Pick a directory or index you like and tell your browser to go to the index or directory's home page.**

    After you get there, you can choose between two approaches:

    - **The index approach:** If a Search box is available, type some likely keywords in the box and click Search. After a perhaps long delay (the Web is pretty big), an index page is returned with links to pages that match your keywords.
    - **The directory approach:** If you see a list of links to topic areas, click a topic area of interest, beginning at a general topic. Each page then has links to pages that get more and more specific until they link to actual pages that are likely to be of interest.

3. **Refine and repeat your search until you find the information you're seeking.**

Locating Popular Search Engines

The following sections introduce you to a variety of search engines from those that deal with a broad range of information to those that deal with a more specific topics.

Yahoo!

Yahoo! (yes, the exclamation point is part of the spelling) is the king of the Internet search engines. Start your search at www.yahoo.com, which looks like Figure 3-1. (As with all Web pages, the exact design may have changed by the time you read this book.) Yahoo! lists several categories and subcategories. You can click any of them to see another page that has yet more subcategories and links to actual Web pages. You can click a link to a page if you see one you like, or on a sub-subcategory, and so on. If you know in general but not in detail what you're looking for, clicking up and down through the Yahoo! directory pages is a good way to narrow your search and find pages of interest.

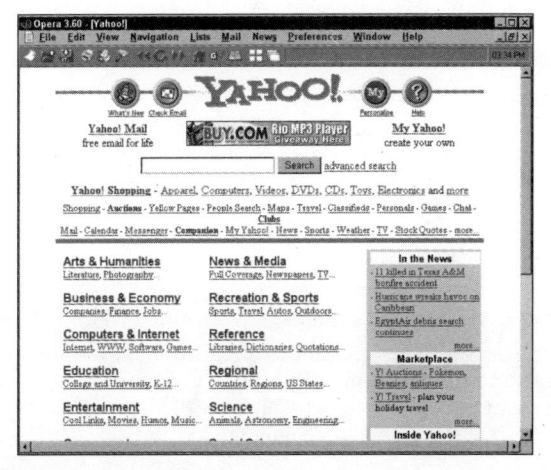

Figure 3-1: Ready to Yahoo!

Yahoo! also lets you search its index by keyword, which is the best way to use it if you have some idea of the title of the page you're looking for. Every Yahoo! screen has a search box near the top in which you can type words you want to find in the Yahoo! entry for pages of interest. Above each entry Yahoo! finds, it reports the category in which it found the entry. Even if the entry isn't quite right, you can click the category to find other related titles, which may do the trick.

> **TIP** If Yahoo! finds hundreds of pages or categories, you should refine your search. One way to do that is to add extra words to make more specific what you're looking for. You can click "advanced search," next to the Search button, to get to the slightly more advanced Yahoo! search page.

Google and AltaVista

Google and AltaVista both have little robots that spend their time merrily visiting Web pages all over the Net and reporting back what they see. These systems have about ten times as many pages as Yahoo!, but finding the one you want can be difficult.

With AltaVista, you can easily refine your search to more exactly target the pages you want to find. After each search, your search terms appear in a box at the top of the page so that you can change them and try again.

Google, at www.google.com, is an index somewhat like AltaVista, but with some extra smarts to make it more likely that pages of interest will show up on the first page of results. The "I'm Feeling Lucky" button searches and takes you directly to the first link, which works when, well, when you're lucky. Google has a couple of other useful features. If you click the "Cached" link on any of the pages that Google finds, it'll show you a copy of the page as of the time that Google indexed it, useful for pages that change often or have disappeared. The "Googlescout" link looks for pages related to that page, often with more useful info.

Other popular search engines

After you surf around Yahoo!, Google, and AltaVista for a while, you may want to check out the competition as well:

- **Excite (**www.excite.com**):** Excite is primarily an index with a "concept search," which is supposed to find relevant pages even if you don't type exactly the same words the pages use.

- **WebCrawler (**www.webcrawler.com**):** A reasonable alternative to AltaVista, WebCrawler is an automated indexer that crawls around the Web cataloging and indexing every page it comes across.

- **Infoseek (**www.infoseek.com**) and GO.com** (www.go.com)**:** Similar to AltaVista, you give Infoseek some keywords to look for, and it finds the pages that match the best. It also has a directory of useful Web pages.

Lots of other Web guides are available, including many specialized guides put together for particular interests (Femina, for example, is a feminist guide, at femina.cybergrrl.com). Yahoo! has a directory of other guides, as well. Starting at the Yahoo! page (www.yahoo.com), choose WWW (which appears under Computers and Internet) and then Searching the Web.

Part 4
Mastering Netiquette

In This Part
- ▶ Cultivating good manners on mailing lists and e-mail
- ▶ Following cybercafé etiquette
- ▶ Designing friendly Web pages

On the Net, you are what you type. The messages you send are the only way that 99 percent of the people you meet on the Net will know you. Sadly, the Great Ladies of Etiquette, such as Emily Post and Amy Vanderbilt, died before the invention of e-mail. Here's what they may have suggested about what to say and, more important, what not to say in electronic mail. This chapter offers you tips for minding your *netiquette* — Internet etiquette.

Read Before You Write

The moment you get your new Internet account, you may have an overwhelming urge to begin sending out lots of messages right away. Don't do it! Read mailing lists, Web pages, and other Net resources for a while before you send anything out. By doing so, you'll figure out where best to send your messages, which makes it both more likely that you will contact people who are interested in what you say and less likely that you will annoy people by bothering them with irrelevancies or by sending something to an inappropriate place. If you see a FAQ (Frequently Asked Questions) section, read it to see whether your question has already been answered.

Advice you probably didn't hear from your mom

E-mail is a funny hybrid, something between a phone call (or voice mail) and a letter. On one hand, it's quick and usually informal; on the other hand, because e-mail is written rather than spoken, you don't see a person's facial expressions or hear her tone of voice.

A few words of advice:

- **When you send a message, watch the tone of your language.**
- **Don't use all capital letters — it looks like you're SHOUTING.**
- **If someone sends you an incredibly obnoxious and offensive message, as likely as not it's a mistake or a joke gone awry:** In particular, be on the lookout for failed sarcasm. Sometimes it helps to put in a :-) (called a *smiley*), which means, "This is a joke." (Try leaning way over to the left if you don't see why it's a smile.) In some communities, notably CompuServe, <g> or <grin> serves the same purpose. Here's a typical example:

    People who don't believe that we are all part of a warm, caring community who love and support each other are no better than rabid dogs and should be hunted down and shot. :-)

Check Your Spelling and Punctuation

Many Net users feel that because Net messages are short and informal, spelling and grammar don't count. If you feel that wey, theirs' not much wee can do abowt it. We think that a sloppy, misspelled message is like a big grease stain on your shirt — your friends will know that it's you, but people who don't know you will conclude that you don't know how to dress yourself.

> **TIP:** Many mail programs have spell checkers. Eudora Pro (the commercial version of Eudora) checks your spelling after you click the dictionary icon (the ABC one) on the toolbar or choose Edit⇨Check Spelling from the menu; in Netscape 4.x, which also comes with a spell checker, you choose Tools⇨Check Spelling from the menu. In Outlook Express, you can elect, via the Options menu, to have your outgoing messages checked or choose Tools⇨Spelling to check any message in progress. In Pine, you check your spelling by pressing Ctrl+T. Although spell checkers aren't perfect, at least they ensure that your messages consist of 100 percent genuine words.

Don't Abuse Mailing Lists

Signing up for a mailing list is a cool thing. Still, however, a classic way to look like a klutz is to send to the list itself a message asking to be added to or taken off a list; all the people on the list have to read the message, but it doesn't actually get the sender subscribed or taken off. Subscribe and unsubscribe requests go to the list server program in a particular format or, in the case of lists that aren't automated, to the list owner.

When you first subscribe to a mailing list, you usually get back a long message about how this particular list operates and how to unsubscribe if you want. Read this message. Save this message. Before you go telling other people on the list how to behave, read the rules again. Some officious newbie, newly subscribed to JAZZ-L, began flaming the list and complaining about the off-topic threads. JAZZ-L encourages this kind of discussion — it says so right in the introduction to the list. Can't say as how she made herself really welcome with that move.

> **TIP:** Avoid trying to sound smart. When you do, the result is usually its opposite. Each message you post to a list goes to the entire list. If you're going to participate, find a constructive way to do so.

Edit Yourself

When you're posting to a mailing list, remember that your audience is the entire world, made up of people of all ethnicities and races speaking different languages and representing different cultures. Work hard to represent yourself and your culture well. Avoid name-calling and disparaging comments about other peoples and places. Read several times through whatever you intend to post before you send it. We have seen inadvertent typos change the intended meaning of a message to its complete opposite.

> **⚠ WARNING**
>
> ### Potshots aren't for hot shots
>
> Sooner or later, you see something that cries out for a cheap shot. Sooner or later, someone sends you something you shouldn't have seen and you want to pass it on. Don't do it. Resist cheap shots and proliferating malice. The Net has plenty of jerks — don't be another one.

Don't Embarrass Someone

Yes, it's true, people sometimes make dumb moves when they post to a mailing list. Don't compound their mistakes, however, by posting additional messages complaining about it. Either delete the message and forget about it or respond privately, by e-mail addressed only to the person, not to the mailing list. The entire mailing list probably doesn't want to hear your advice to the person who blew it.

Keep Your Signature Short

All mail programs let you have a signature, a file that gets added to the end of each mail or news message you send. The signature is supposed to contain something to identify you. Snappy quotes have quickly become common, to add that personal touch.

Some people's signatures get way out of hand, going on for 100 lines of "ASCII art," long quotations, extensive disclaimers, and other allegedly interesting stuff. Although this type of signature may seem cute the first time or two, it quickly gets tedious and marks you as a total newbie.

> **REMEMBER:** Keep your signature to four lines or fewer. All the experienced Net users do.

Don't Get Attached

Attachments are a useful way to send files by e-mail. But they work only if the person on the receiving end has a program that can read the files you're sending. For example, if you send a WordPerfect document to someone who doesn't have a word-processing program, the file is unreadable. Ditto for graphics files, sound files, and other files you may want to send around. Indeed, some older mail systems can't handle attachments at all. Ask first before sending an attachment.

The same rule applies for sending formatted e-mail. Newer e-mail programs let you use boldface, italics, and other formatting, but formatted messages are readable only if you have a matching e-mail program. On older programs, formatted messages contain so many formatting characters that the text is unreadable. Don't send formatted messages to mailing lists.

Don't Flame

When you're sending mail, keep in mind that someone reading it will have no idea of what you intended to say — just what you did say. Subtle sarcasm and irony are almost impossible to use in e-mail and usually come across as annoying or dumb instead. (If you're an extremely superb writer, you can disregard this advice — but don't say that we didn't warn you.)

For some reason, it's easy to get VERY, VERY UPSET ABOUT SOMETHING SOMEONE SAYS ON THE NET. (See, it happens even to us.) Sometimes it's something you find on the Web, and sometimes it's personal e-mail. You may be tempted to shoot a message right back telling that person what a doofus he is. Guess what? He will almost certainly shoot back. This type of overstated outrage is so common that it has its own name: *flaming*.

Now and then, flaming is fun if you're certain that the recipient will take it in good humor, but it's always unnecessary. For one thing, e-mail messages always come across as crabbier than the author intended; for another, crabbing back will hardly make the person more reasonable.

When you get a message so offensive that you just have to reply, stick it back in your electronic inbox and wait until after lunch. Then, don't flame back. The sender probably didn't realize how the message would look. In about 20 years of using electronic mail, we can testify that we have never, ever, regretted not sending an angry message (although we have regretted sending a few — ouch).

Another possibility to keep in the back of your mind is that forging e-mail return addresses is technically not difficult. If you get a totally off-the-wall message from someone that seems out of character for that person, somebody else may have forged it as a prank.

Don't Send Chain Letters or Spam

Sending a chain letter on the Net is easy: Just click the Forward button, type a few names, and send your letter off. It's a lousy idea. We have never, ever gotten a chain letter that was worth passing along. A bunch of classic chain letters have been circulating around the Net for a decade (with topics like phantom viruses, nonexistent modem taxes, the overpriced recipe that isn't, and a way that you won't make money fast). Regardless of where they come from, even if they seem to be for a good cause, please just throw them away.

One of the least pleasant online innovations in recent years is *spamming,* or sending the same message — usually selling something that was rather dubious in the first place — to as many e-mail addresses as possible. This practice is annoying, illegal in some places, and the *spammer* (the person who sends the spam) is usually liable for her ISP's costs in cleaning it up. An increasing number of ISPs offer e-mail filtering, and most recipients presume that anything advertised by spam must be fraudulent.

Don't Be a Glutton

Unbelievable amounts of material are on the Net: programs, documents, pictures, megabyte after megabyte of swell stuff — all free for the taking. You can download it all. Don't. Go ahead and take whatever you're likely to use, but don't download entire directories full of stuff or leave your computer online for hours at a time "just in case."

Your ISP sets its charges based on the resources a typical user uses. A single user can use a substantial fraction of the provider's Net connection by sucking down files continuously for hours at a time. ISPs typically "overcommit" their Net connection by a factor of three or so. That is, if every user tried to transfer data at full speed at the same time, it would require three times as fast a connection as the ISP has. Because real users transfer for a while and then read what's on-screen for a while, sharing the connection among all the users works out okay. (The ISP is not cheating you by using this method; it's a sensible way to provide access at a reasonable cost. Although you can get guaranteed connection performance if you want it, the price is horrifying.) If users begin using several more connections than the ISP budgeted for, prices will go up.

> Most ISPs offer unlimited connect-time per month, but don't leave your computer connected if you're not using it. Most Net software packages have a time-out feature that hangs up if no data is transferred to or from the Net for a specified period. We leave ours set to 15 minutes on our dial-up connections; otherwise, other users get a busy signal when they try to connect.

Bone Up on Cybercafé Etiquette

Cybercafés are new, and our parents never had the opportunity to teach us the ins and outs. As experienced Internet users, however, we have a few tips to help you ease your way into the scene and not embarrass yourself completely:

- **Don't gawk over other people's shoulders:** Okay, we understand that you're curious — that's why you're here, to find out about this stuff. Great. Cool. Rent some time, and get some help. But don't stand over other people's shoulders reading their screen. It's rude.

- ✔ **Do clean up after yourself:** We mean not just the trash around your computer but also the trash you probably left on the computer. Many folks don't seem to be aware that most mailer programs keep copies of messages that are sent. If you don't want someone to read your mail, make sure that you find the sent-message folder and delete your mail. Then take the next step and empty the trash. We have found all kinds of interesting goodies we're sure that the sender wouldn't have wanted to share.

- ✔ **Don't order stuff from a public PC:** Normally, we think that ordering stuff over the Web or by e-mail is perfectly safe — much safer than handing your credit card to some waiter you've never met! Some shopping sites store information about you, however (including your mailing address and payment info), in a file on your computer. This arrangement works perfectly when you are ordering from your own computer — you don't have to type all that info when you visit the site the next time to place an order. When you order stuff at a cybercafé, however, this personal information may be stored on the cybercafé's computer instead. Better not chance it.

Make Your Web Site User Friendly

Most ISPs let you put your own private pages up on the World Wide Web. If you decide to do so, remember that what you put on your Web page is all that most people will know about you. With that in mind, here are a few suggestions for making your Web site accessible:

- **Keep your pictures small:** Most people who look at your Web page are connected by using a dial-up line and a modem, which means that big pictures take a long time to load. If your home page contains a full-page picture that takes 12½ minutes to load, you may as well have posted a Keep Out sign. Keep the pictures small enough that the page loads in a reasonable amount of time. If you have a huge picture that you think is wonderful, put a small "thumbnail" version of it on your home page and make it a link to the full picture for people with the time and interest to look at the big version.

- **Keep your pages small:** Small pages that fit on a screen or two work better than large pages. Small pages are easier to read, and they load faster. If you have 12 screens full of stuff to put on your Web page, break up your page into 5 or 6 separate pages with links among them. A well-designed set of small pages makes finding stuff easier than does one big page because the links can direct readers to what they want to find.

- **Link to interesting and unusual sites:** No Web page (or set of Web pages) is complete without some links to the author's other favorite pages. For some reason, every new user's Web page used to have a link to www.whitehouse.gov and maybe to Yahoo!, Netscape, and a few other sites that every Net user already knows about. Cool Web sites give you links to interesting pages you don't already know about.

- **Make your Web site multi-browser ready:** Whenever you create a new Web page, look at it with as many Web browsers as possible. Yes, most people use some version of Netscape or Internet Explorer, but Prodigy and AOL users (over 10 million possible visitors to your site) use the browsers that come with those services, many people use Opera and other lesser known browsers, and users with dial-up shell connections use the text-only browser Lynx. Take a look at your pages to make sure that they're at least legible regardless of which browser people are using.

- **Don't be too free with personal information:** Don't put information on your Web page that you don't want everyone in the world to know. In particular, don't include your home address and phone number. We know at least one person who received an unexpected phone call from someone she met on the Net and wasn't too pleased about it. Why would Net users need this information, anyway? They can send you e-mail!

Part 5
Welcoming You to the Windows Millennium

● ●

In This Part

▶ Understanding what Windows Me is and what it does

▶ Finding out how Windows Me affects your current programs

▶ Deciding whether you should upgrade to Windows Me

● ●

One way or another, you've probably already heard about Microsoft Windows. Everybody who's anybody talks breezily about Windows, the Internet, and the World Wide Web. Weird code words, like www.vw.com, stare out cryptically from magazine, newspaper, and television advertisements. To help you play catch-up in the world of Windows, this part previews the basics of the latest version of Windows, called *Windows Me,* and shows how Windows Me works with your older Windows programs. (***Note:*** As is the case with any preview, the final product may vary slightly from the information you read here.)

What Are Windows and Windows Me?

Windows is just another piece of software, like the zillions of others lining the store shelves. But it's not a program in the normal sense — something that lets you write letters or lets your coworkers play Bozark the Destroyer over the office network after everybody else goes home. Rather, Windows controls the way you work with your computer.

- **Windows software dumps the typewriter feel and updates the *look* of computers:** Windows replaces the words and numbers with pictures and fun buttons. It's smooth and shiny, like an expensive, new coffeemaker.

- **Windows software looks and acts differently from traditional computer programs, so understanding it can take a few days:** After all, you probably couldn't make perfect coffee the first day, either.

- **Windows Me is the most powerful version of Windows software — software that's been updated many times since starting to breathe in January 1985:** It's short for Windows *Millennium*, but Microsoft labels it "Windows Me." We don't know why. Nobody else likes the name, either.

- **Windows software is big enough and powerful enough to be called an *operating system*, according to programmer types:** That's because Windows "operates" your computer. Most computer users, however, call Windows lots of other names, including some that our editor won't let us publish here.

Windows 2000 **is Microsoft's biggest, most powerful version of Windows:** Stronger and more full-featured, Windows 2000 is favored mostly by large office networks so all the computers can talk to each other. In fact, Microsoft eventually plans to discontinue its Windows Me line in favor of its Windows 2000 series. (That means Windows 2000 also gets its own book, *Windows 2000 Professional For Dummies,* written by Andy Rathbone and Sharon Crawford, and published by IDG Books Worldwide, Inc.)

Windows 2000 isn't the replacement for Windows 98, even though its name sounds like it's the logical next step: No, Windows 2000 is the latest version of Windows NT, the corporate version of Windows used for networking. Windows Me — also known as Windows Millennium — is the replacement for Windows 98, even though the two names have nothing in common.

What Does Windows Do?

Like the mother with the whistle in the lunch court, Windows controls all the parts of your computer. You turn on your computer, start Windows, and start running programs. Each program runs in its own little *window* on-screen, as shown in Figure 5-1. Yet Windows keeps things safe, even if the programs start throwing food at each other.

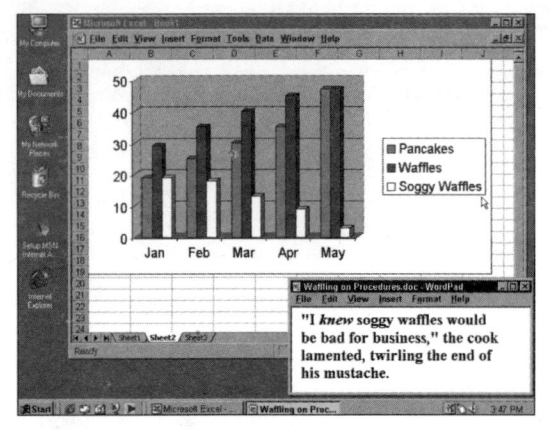

Figure 5-1: Each program has its own window on the world.

Windows gets its name from all the cute little windows on-screen. Each window shows some information: a picture, perhaps, or a program that you're running. You can put several windows on-screen at the same time and jump from window to window, visiting different programs.

Some people say that colorful windows and pictures make Windows easier to use; others say that Windows is a little too arty. To write a letter in Windows Me, for example, do you select the picture of the notepad, the quill, or the clipboard? And what potential problems can emerge with the icons of the spinning globe and the bomb?

- ✔ **A computer environment that uses little pictures and symbols is called a *graphical user interface,* or *GUI* (pronounced *gooey,* believe it or not):** Pictures require more computing horsepower than letters and numbers, so Windows Me requires a relatively powerful computer. (You can find a list of its requirements later in this part.)

- ✔ **When the word *Windows* starts with a capital letter, it refers to the Windows program; when the word *windows* starts with a lowercase letter, it refers to windows you see on-screen.**

> **REMEMBER:** Because Windows uses graphics, it's much easier to use than to describe. To tell someone how to move through a Windows document you say, "Click in the vertical scroll bar beneath the scroll box." Those directions sound awfully weird, but after you've done it, you'll say, "Oh, is that all? Golly!" (Plus, you can still press the PgDn key in Windows. You don't have to "click in the vertical scroll bar beneath the scroll box" if you don't want to.)

With Windows Me, your desktop doesn't have to look like a typewritten page *or* a desktop. Now, it can look just like an Internet Web page. In fact, the chameleon-like Windows Me can run like a Web page, using the "Classic Windows 95" settings, or you can customize it with any combination — all of which introduce many more ways for things to go wrong.

How Does Windows Me Affect My Older Programs?

Windows Me can still run most of your older Windows programs, too, thank goodness. So after upgrading to Windows Me, you won't have to immediately buy expensive new software. It runs almost all Windows 98 and Windows 95 programs, as well as many Windows 3.1 programs. If you're finally upgrading from an old computer that uses DOS, Windows Me can probably still run your old DOS programs. (Your dusty old computer probably won't have enough oomph to run Windows Me, but chances are you wanted a new one, anyway.)

> When people say Windows Me is *backward compatible,* that just means it can run software that was written for older versions of Windows. You can still run most Windows 95 and Windows 3.1 software on Windows Me, for example, as well as most DOS software. (Don't even think about running Macintosh software, though.)

However, most programs from the Windows 3.0 generation or earlier simply can't keep up with Windows Me. You just can't take Windows Me, install it onto your five-year-old computer and expect it to run well. No; Windows Me is a big operating system for a big computer. You'll probably have to buy a new one or add bigger shoulders to your older one. (In computer language, big shoulders translate to a faster CPU chip, more memory, a larger hard drive, and a CD-ROM drive.) Unfortunately, adding bigger shoulders often costs more than buying a new PC.

Should I Bother Using Windows Me?

Windows 95 and Windows 98 users are elbowing each other nervously by the water cooler and whispering the Big Question: Why bother buying Windows Me, going through the hassle of installing it, and learning all its new programs? Here's why: Windows Me comes pre-installed on most new computers, so many people are simply stuck with it. Also, Windows Me offers quite a few improvements over earlier versions.

Basically, the upgrade question boils down to this answer: If your computer frequently crashes when using Windows 95 or Windows 98, it may be time to upgrade. But if you're happy with your current computer setup, don't bother. After all, why buy new tires if your old ones still have some life left?

Upgrading from Windows 95

Upgrading from Windows 95? Then you'll find Windows Me easier to install. Plus, it handles files faster and more efficiently on today's powerhouse PCs.

- **Windows Me can automatically run background maintenance tasks to keep itself "tuned up" and ready to run:** If you have access to the Internet, Windows Me can diagnose itself to see whether it's up to date, and then automatically grab the latest files it needs to keep running smoothly.

- **Technolusters who like the latest and greatest gadgets will like the new "TV Tuner" programs for watching TV on their monitors (provided you shell out a hundred bucks or so for a TV card):** Or, if your desk is big enough, splurge on another monitor. Windows Me lets you arrange your desktop across both monitors, doubling your workspace. Whoopee!

- **If you're an Internet devotee, you'll like the way Windows Me wraps itself around Microsoft's Web browser, Internet Explorer:** Not only can you make your computer look like a Web page, but you can also have parts of Web pages embedded in your desktop and running in the background — where the boss can't notice 'em as much.

- **Finally, Windows makes the Internet act more like a television, with easily switchable — and customizable — Channels:** You'll find Channels for Disney, America Online, Warner Brothers, and other large corporate conglomerations.

Upgrading from Windows 3.1

Windows 3.1 users who skipped Windows 95 will be pleasantly surprised: They won't have to point and click as much to find files and start programs. For example, Windows Me remembers the names of files or programs you've recently used and stores their names in a special spot. Do you want to load the file again? Just click on the file's name from the pop-up list — no wading through menus or opening programs: White-gloved Windows Me opens the car door and lets you start moving immediately.

You see lots more little buttons with pictures on them — *icons* — used in Windows Me programs. You don't know what the icon with the little butterfly picture is supposed to do? Then just rest your mouse pointer over the icon; after a few seconds, a message often pops up on-screen, explaining the butterfly button's role among the fields of Windows. The most helpful messages appear when you rest the pointer over the unlabeled buttons that hang out along the tops of programs, like word processors and spreadsheets — in their *toolbar* areas.

Windows Me allows longer filenames, just like Windows 95 and Windows 98. After 15 years of frustration, PC users can call their files something more descriptive than RPT45.TXT. In fact, Windows offers you 255 characters to describe your creations.

- **Windows Me can help you upgrade your computer with its upgraded "Plug and Play" concept:** A new Windows Me "Wizard" keeps better track of the parts inside your computer and can alert you when internal brawls start. Better yet, it prevents many brawls from even starting by making sure that two computer parts aren't assigned the same areas of your computer's memory.

- **Windows Me automates many computing chores:** To install a program, for example, just push the floppy disk (or compact disc) into the drive and click the Control Panel's Add/Remove Programs button. Windows searches all your drives for the installation program and runs it automatically. Windows Me can automatically search for any new hardware you've installed as well, recognizing quite a few of the most popular upgrades.

- **Windows Me can format floppy disks in the background so that you can continue playing your card game:** The card game FreeCell is an incredibly delicious time-waster.

Upgrading from Windows 98

Here's the ugly truth about Windows Me that you may not hear anyplace else. Windows Me is really just a slightly polished version of Windows 98. Although Microsoft gave it a face lift, Windows Me really acts almost identically to its cousin.

The big difference? Microsoft changed lots of the icons so they look like its other, corporate-level program called Windows 2000. The changes are more than cosmetic, too. Windows Me makes it easier to work with today's digital cameras by including a video editor. The Media Player's been enhanced to tune in Internet radio stations, create categorized playlists of your MP3s, audio CDs, and video clips. In short, it's competing with RealAudio, WinAmp, and other third-party programs catering to today's multimedia-craving users.

Some people will be excited by these new-tech changes. Others don't bother installing them, because they prefer the third-party programs. And others will wonder whether Windows Me is even worth the upgrade in the first place. Only you can decide.

Bracing Yourself (And Your Computer) for Windows Me

With Windows, everything happens at the same time. Its many different parts run around like hamsters with an open cage door. Programs cover each other up on-screen. They overlap corners, hiding each other's important parts. Occasionally, they simply disappear.

- ✔ **Windows software may be accommodating, but that can cause problems, too:** For example, Windows Me often offers more than three different ways for you to perform the same computing task. Don't bother memorizing each command. Just choose one method that works for you and stick with it.

- ✔ **Windows Me runs best on a powerful new computer with the key words *Pentium, Pentium Pro, Pentium II, Pentium III,* or *testosterone* somewhere in the description:** Look for as much *RAM* (Random-Access Memory) and as many *gigabytes* as you can afford.

- ✔ **Windows Me can easily eat up 300MB of space, depending on how much of it you choose to install:** Your Windows Me programs can eat up even more space. Nobody will laugh if you buy a 8 gigabyte or larger hard drive for Windows Me and your Windows Me programs.

- ✔ **Windows Me benefits from a CD-ROM drive:** Without a CD-ROM drive you won't be able to use most of today's programs. In fact, buy one that can both read and write to CD-R compact discs.

Table 5-1 compares what Windows Me asks for on the side of the box with what you *really* need before it works well.

Table 5-1		What Windows Me Requires
Requirements Politely Touted by Microsoft	*What You Really Need*	*Why?*
A 486 66MHz microprocessor	A Pentium II	While at the store, compare Windows Me running on different computers. The faster the computer, the less time you spend waiting for Windows Me to do something exciting.
16MB of memory (RAM)	At least 32MB of memory	Windows Me crawls across the screen with only 16MB and moves much more comfortably with 32MB. RAM is cheap; if you plan to run several large programs or use WebTV, quickly bump that to 64MB. Power users may want to consider 128MB or more.
195MB of hard disk space	At least 4GB	A full installation of Windows Me requires 300MB; Windows programs quickly rope off their sections of the hard drive, too. Plus, all that sound and video you're going to be grabbing off the Internet and your digital camera will take a whole lotta space. (You'll need at least a gigabyte to watch WebTV.) Don't be afraid to buy a hard disk that's 8GB (eight gigabytes) or larger.

Requirements Politely Touted by Microsoft	What You Really Need	Why?
A 3½-inch high-density disk drive	Same	A few Windows programs still come packaged on high-density, 3½-inch floppy disks. Plus, floppy disks are a handy way to move your files to other computers.
Color VGA card	Super VGA	Because Windows Me tosses so many PCI bus card colorful little boxes on-screen, get a 16-, or accelerated high-resolution 3-D Super 24-bitcolor VGA card with at least 4MB of RAM.
Windows 95, Windows 3.1, Windows for Workgroups (Windows 3.11 or later)	Same	Microsoft is selling Windows Me as an upgrade to its existing products. If you're not upgrading from an earlier version of Windows, you need to buy the "complete," more expensive version of Windows Me.

(continued)

Table 5-1 *(continued)*

Requirements Politely Touted by Microsoft	What You Really Need	Why?
Miscellaneous	A 15-inch monitor or larger	The bigger your monitor, the bigger your desktop: Your windows won't overlap so much. Unfortunately, super-large monitors are super-expensive.
Miscellaneous	CD-ROM or DVD drive	You may be able to find Windows Me on disks, but installation is much easier from a compact disc than from handfuls of floppy disks. (A DVD drive can also read normal CDs, so it'll work fine.)
Miscellaneous	Modem	You don't need a modem, but if your computer isn't on a network, you need a modem to dial up the online services that come packaged with Windows Me, and to play with Internet Explorer.

Buy any IDG Books Windows® Millennium Edition (Windows® Me) Book and get a $2 Publisher's mail-in rebate

To receive your $2 rebate:
1. Complete and submit this form.
2. Send completed form with your cash register receipt with IDG Windows Me Books circled to:

> IDG Books Windows Me Offer
> P.O. Box 5586
> Kalamazoo, MI 49003-5586

*see back side for terms

Name: _____

Address: _____

City: _____

State: _____ Zip: _____

Email address: _____

Store name and city: _____

Book ISBN # _____
(the 5 numbers on bottom of book spine)

**Begins June 15 and ends November 30, 2000
Good on any IDG Windows Millennium
Edition (Windows Me) book**

www.dummies.com   www.idgbooks.com

To receive your $2 rebate:
1. Complete and submit this form.
2. Send completed form with your cash register receipt with IDG Windows Me books circled to:

IDG Books Windows Me Offer
P.O. Box 5586
Kalamazoo, MI 49003-5586

Terms: All requests must be received by 12:00am, December 31, 2000. Cash register receipt must be dated June 15, 2000 to November 30, 2000. $2 rebate limited to one per name, address, or household. Use of multiple addresses to obtain additional refunds constitutes fraud. Incomplete or incorrect submissions will not be honored. Offer good only in Continental U.S.A. Void where prohibited by law. All submissions and receipts become the exclusive property of IDG Books Worldwide, Inc. This offer may not be published in any refunding magazine or elsewhere without IDG Books' prior written permission. Allow 6–8 weeks for delivery. IDG Books is not responsible for lost, late, illegible or incomplete orders or postage-due, damaged or separated mail. This offer cannot be combined with any other offers.

Offer good on the following books only:

Microsoft® Windows® Me For Dummies®	0-7645-0735-4	$19.99
Microsoft® Windows® Me For Dummies® Quick Reference	0-7645-0730-3	$12.99
Teach Yourself Microsoft® Windows® Me	0-7645-3488-2	$19.99
Alan Simpson's Microsoft® Windows® Me Bible	0-7645-3489-0	$34.99
MORE Microsoft® Windows® Me For Dummies®	0-7645-0734-6	$22.99
Microsoft® Windows® Me Secrets®	0-7645-3493-9	$39.99
Microsoft® Windows® Me Simplified®	0-7645-3494-7	$24.99
Teach Yourself Microsoft® Windows® Me VISUALLY™	0-7645-3495-5	$29.99
Master Microsoft® Windows® Me VISUALLY™	0-7645-3496-3	$34.99
CliffsNotes Making Microsoft® Windows® Me Work for You	0-7645-8645-9	$ 8.99
Microsoft® Windows® Movie Maker For Dummies®	0-7645-0741-9	$19.99
The Internet For Microsoft® Windows® Me For Dummies®	0-7645-0739-7	$19.99

For questions regarding the shipment of your rebate call 1-877-404-9175.

Buy any Dummies® Book and get a $2 Publisher's mail-in rebate

To receive your $2 rebate:
1. Complete and submit this form.
2. Send completed form with your cash register receipt with Dummies® Book circled to:

Dummies® Book Rebate Offer
P.O. Box 5585
Kalamazoo, MI 49003-5585

*see back side for terms

Name: _____

Address: _____

City: _____

State: _____ Zip: _____

Email address: _____

Store name and city: _____

Book ISBN # _____
(the 5 numbers on bottom of book spine)
*excludes Windows 98 For Dummies

**Begins June 15 and ends November 30, 2000
Good on any Dummies® Book**

IDG BOOKS WORLDWIDE

For a complete list of Dummies® Books, visit **www.dummies.com**

To receive your $2 rebate:
1. Complete and submit this form.
2. Send completed form with your cash register receipt with Dummies® Book circled to:

Dummies® Book Rebate
P.O. Box 5585
Kalamazoo, MI 49003-5585

Terms: All requests must be received by 12:00am, December 31, 2000. Cash register receipt must be dated June 15, 2000 to November 30, 2000. $2 rebate limited to one per name, address, or household. Use of multiple addresses to obtain additional refunds constitutes fraud. Incomplete or incorrect submissions will not be honored. Offer good only in Continental U.S.A. Void where prohibited by law. All submissions and receipts become the exclusive property of IDG Books Worldwide, Inc. This offer may not be published in any refunding magazine or elsewhere without IDG Books' prior written permission. Allow 6–8 weeks for delivery. IDG Books is not responsible for lost, late, illegible or incomplete orders or postage-due, damaged or separated mail. This offer cannot be combined with other offers. Windows® 98 For Dummies® is not included in this rebate offer.

For questions regarding the shipment of your rebate call 1-877-404-9175.